THE YOUNG PIANIST'S LIBRARY

No. 1B

FROM BACH TO BARTOK
ORIGINAL PIANO PIECES BY THE MASTERS

VOLUME B

Selected and Edited by
DENES AGAY

Titles in approximate order of difficulty		Page
WALTZ	Dmitri Kabalevsky	23
MUSETTE	From Johann Sebastian Bach's "Notebook for Anna Magdalena"	3
SONG OF THE VAGABOND	Béla Bartók	24
GERMAN DANCE	Joseph Haydn	11
CARNIVAL	Francois Couperin	6
MINUET	Johann Sebastian Bach	2
SCHERZINO	Georg Philipp Telemann	8
MINUET	Wolfgang Amadeus Mozart	12
ANDANTE GRAZIOSO (from Sonatina in G)	Joseph Haydn	10
AIR	Wolfgang Amadeus Mozart	13
MARCH	Dmitri Shostakovich	22
MELODY	Robert Schumann	16
HAPPY STORY	Robert Volkmann	20
MINUET	George Frederick Handel	4
ANGLOISE	From Leopold Mozart's "Notebook for Wolfgang"	9
BOURREE	George Frederick Handel	5
ITALIAN SONG	Peter Ilyitch Tchaikovsky	18
RIGAUDON	Louis-Claude Daquin	7
LÄNDLER	Franz Schubert	19
ON THE SWING	Alexander Gretchaninoff	21
THE WILD HORSEMAN	Robert Schumann	17
THREE COUNTRY DANCES	Ludwig van Beethoven	14

© 1960 WARNER BROS. INC. (Renewed)
All Rights Reserved

2 - *The Young Pianist's Library*

MINUET

JOHANN SEBASTIAN BACH

Allegretto

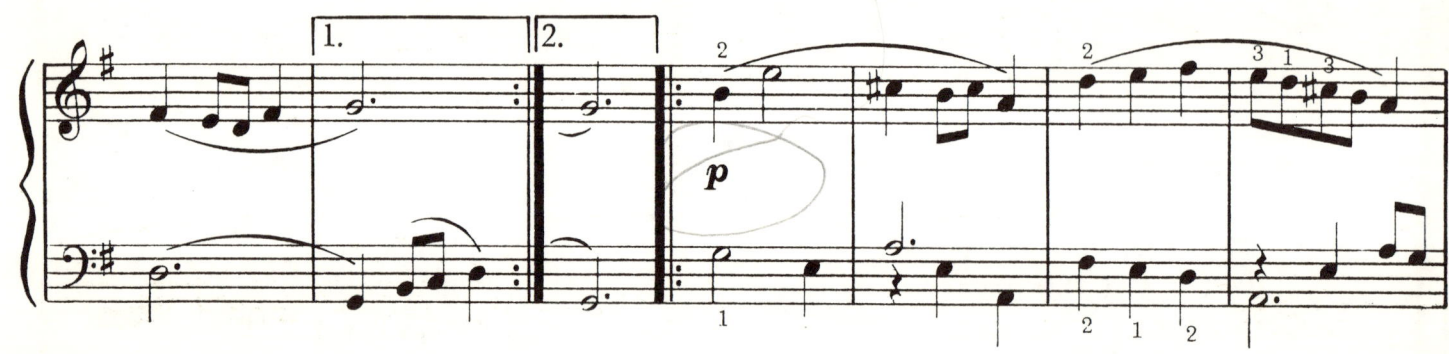
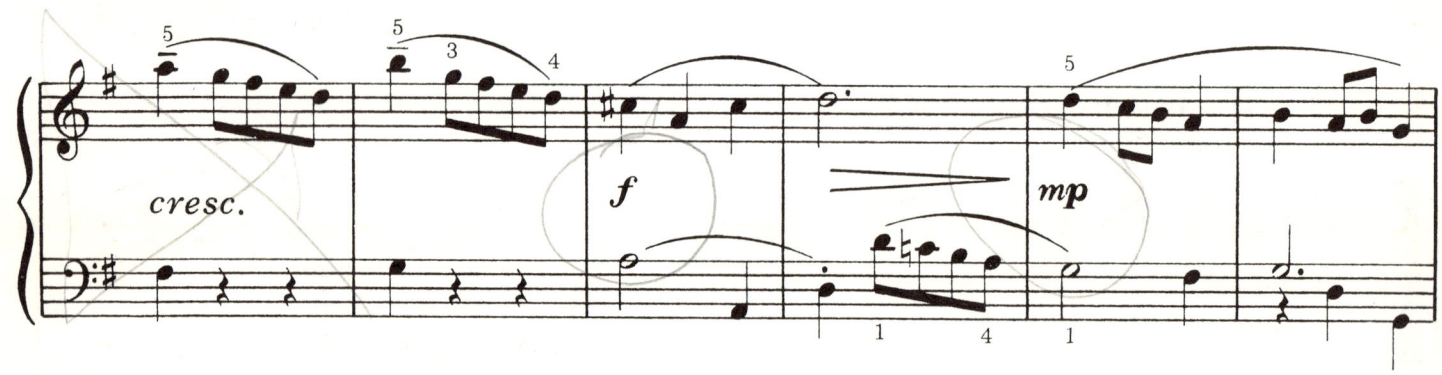

MUSETTE

From Johann Sebastian Bach's "Notebook for Anna Magdalena"

Allegretto

MINUET

GEORGE FREDERICK HANDEL

Andante grazioso

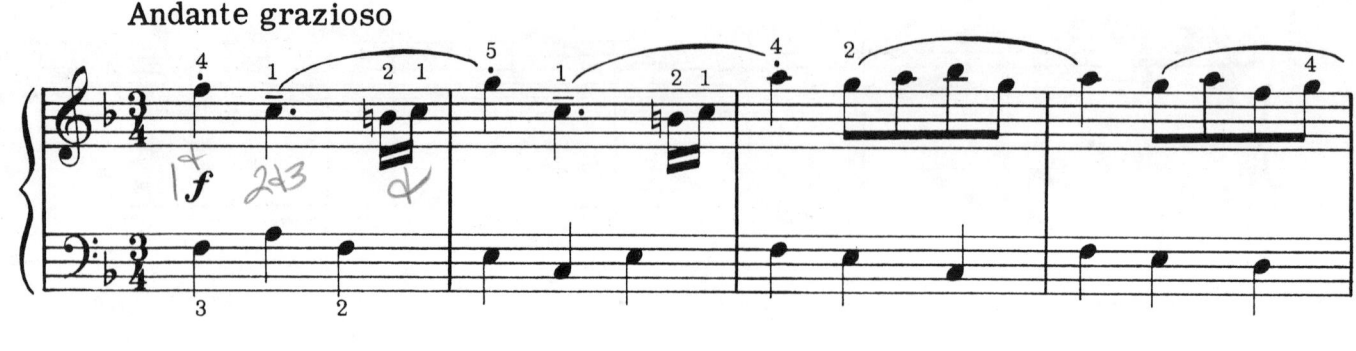

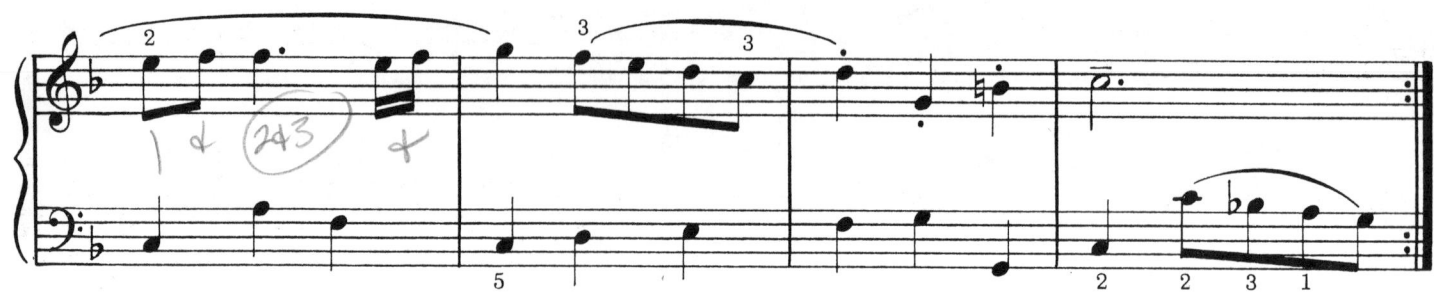

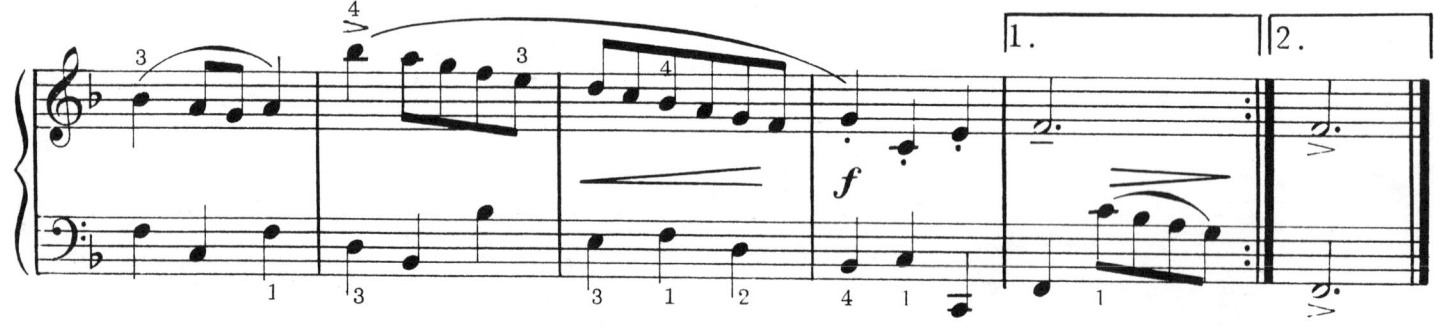

BOURRÉE

GEORGE FREDERICK HANDEL

RIGAUDON

LOUIS-CLAUDE DAQUIN

SCHERZINO

GEORG PHILIPP TELEMANN

Allegretto giocoso

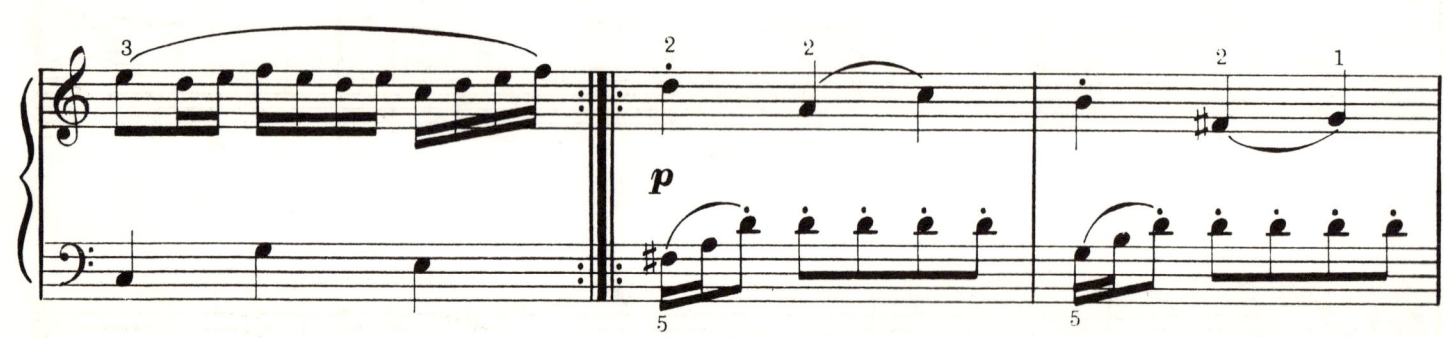

ANGLOISE

From Leopold Mozart's "Notebook for Wolfgang"

ANDANTE GRAZIOSO

(from Sonatina in G)

Feb 3
Hit smooth don't look down!

JOSEPH HAYDN

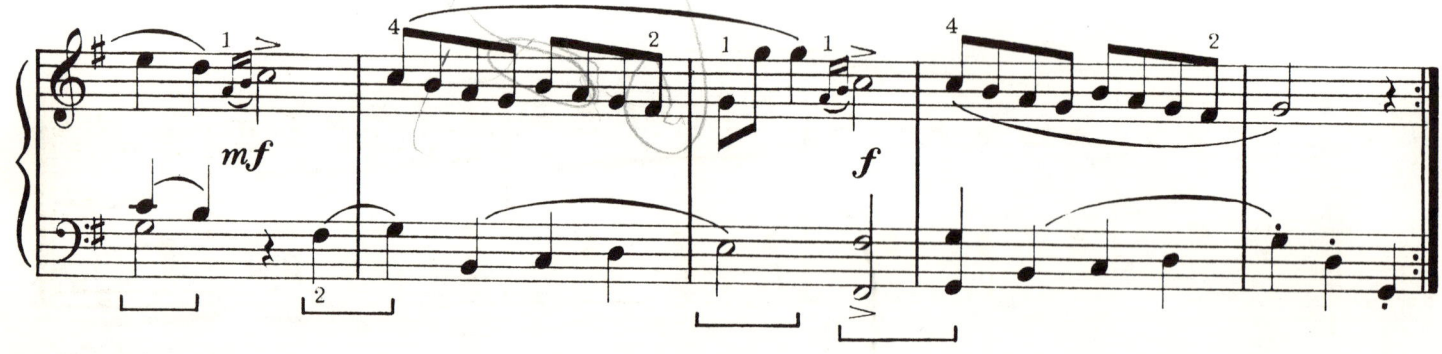

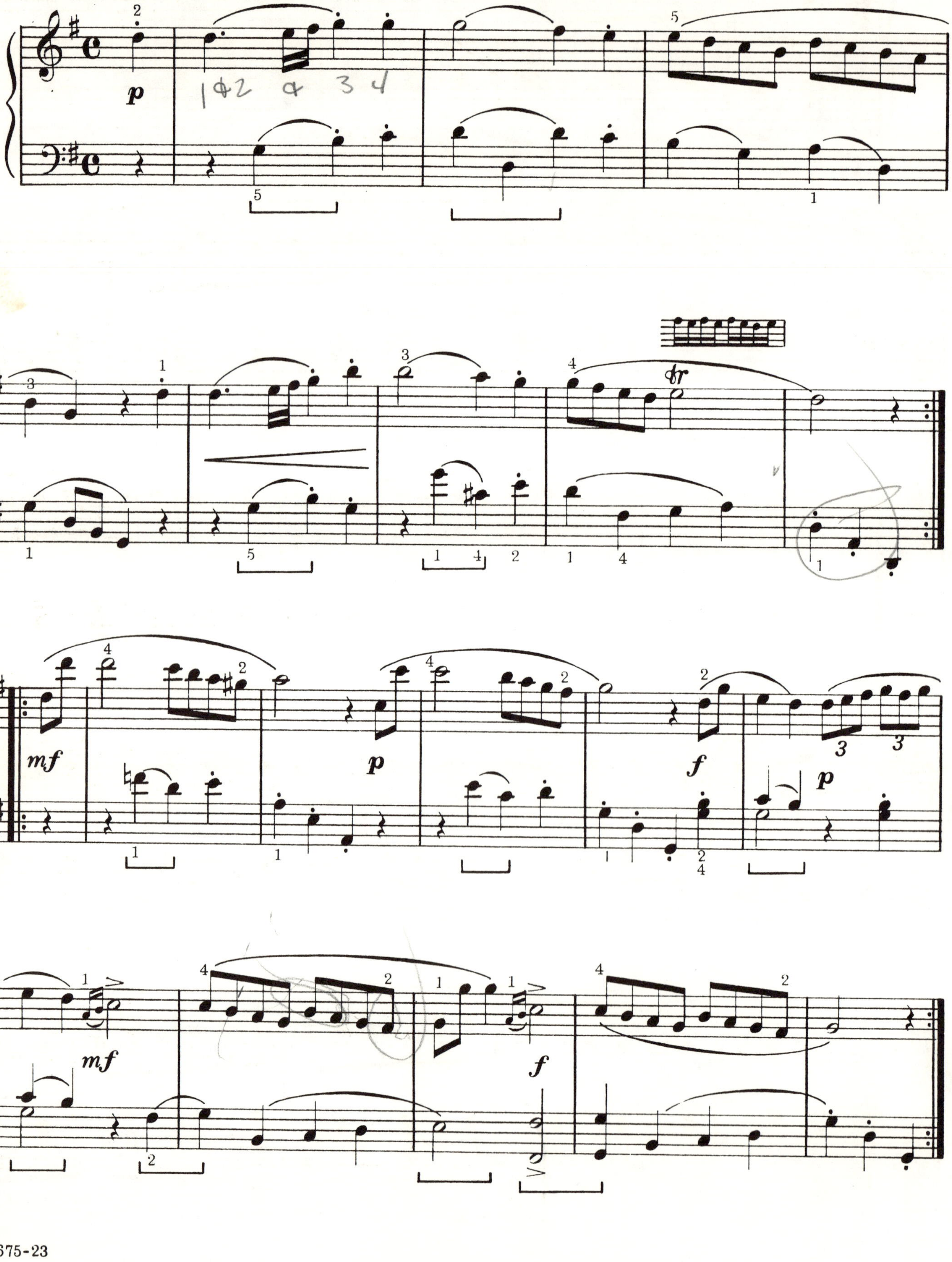

GERMAN DANCE

JOSEPH HAYDN

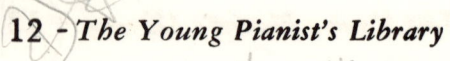

MINUET

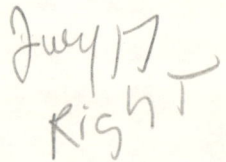

WOLFGANG AMADEUS MOZART

Andantino

AIR

WOLFGANG AMADEUS MOZART

THREE COUNTRY DANCES

LUDWIG VAN BEETHOVEN

MELODY

ROBERT SCHUMANN

Moderato

THE WILD HORSEMAN

ROBERT SCHUMANN

LÄNDLER

Con moto

FRANZ SCHUBERT

20 - *The Young Pianist's Library*

HAPPY STORY

ROBERT VOLKMANN

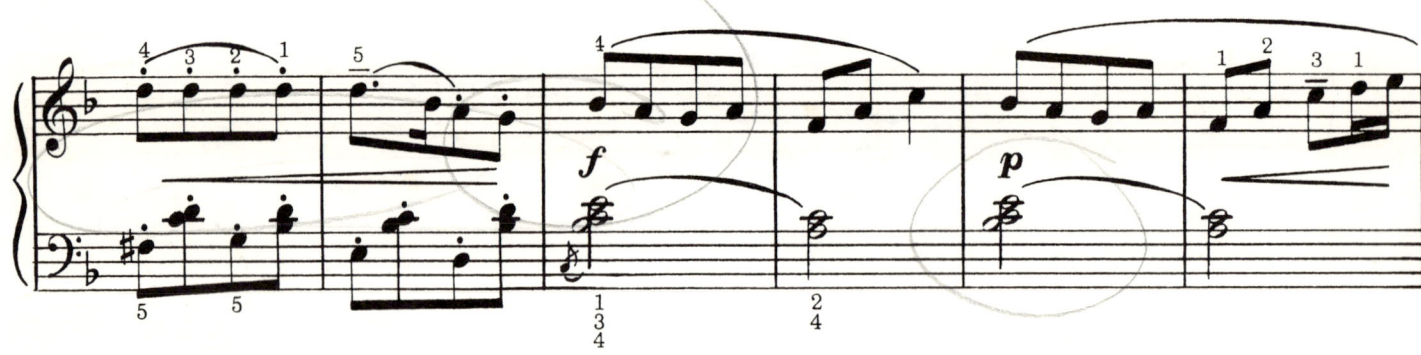

MARCH

DMITRI SHOSTAKOVICH

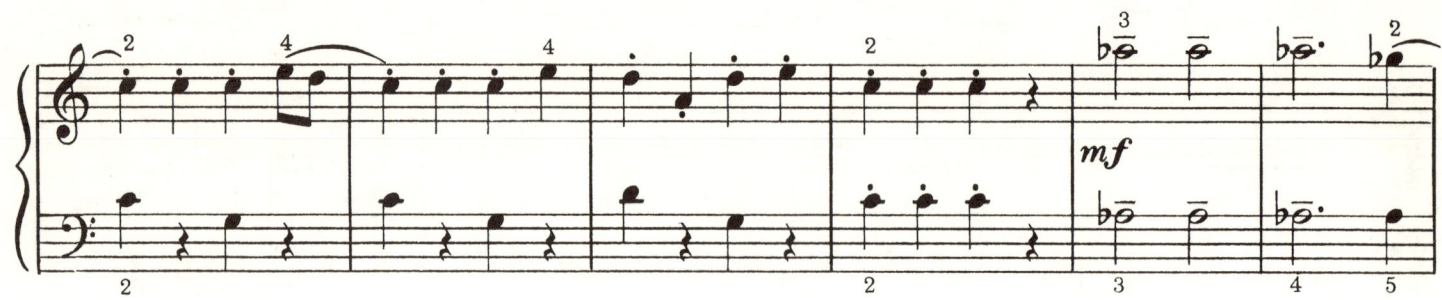

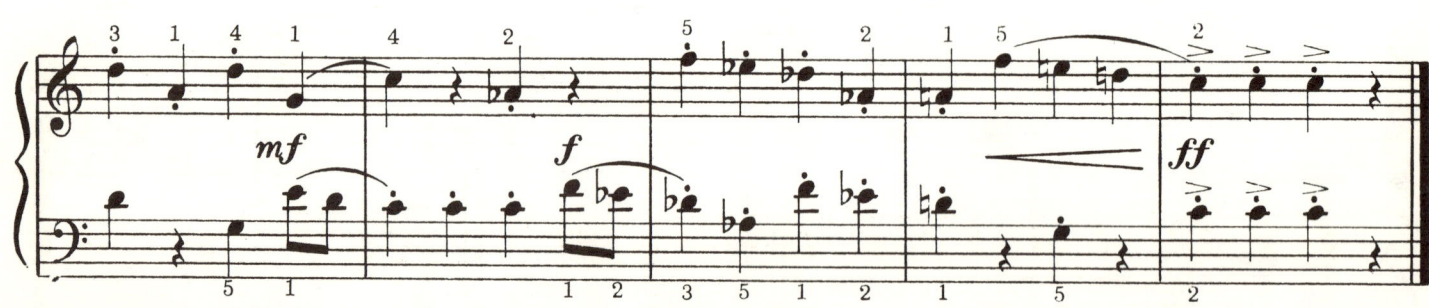

SONG OF THE VAGABOND

BÉLA BARTÓK